# Oma and Opa's Farmhouse

by Carmel Reilly

illustrated by Beth Hughes

Dad helped Reese to pack. Reese was going to Oma and Opa's. They lived on a farm, a long drive away.

"What will I do at the farmhouse? It has been ages since I visited," said Reese.

"Lots of fun things," said Dad. "I promise!"

Dad drove Reese to the farm.

Oma and Opa rushed out of the house. Bomber the dog danced around.

Dad climbed into the car to leave. “I promise to message you lots,” he said. “But I know you will love it here.”

Reese quickly followed Oma into the kitchen.

“What can I do?” asked Reese.

“Opa is checking on the lambs,” said Oma. “He might need some assistance.”

Reese headed out of the old back gate. Chickens and a goose waddled across the grass. A horse and a cow gently leaned over the fence.

Reese could hear Opa's voice in the distance.

"Where are you, Opa?" Reese called timidly.

"In the red shed," he called back.

"Would you like to feed this lamb?" asked Opa. "It takes a bit of practice," he added.

Reese knelt and Opa held the bottle out.

The lamb wriggled and knocked the bottle.

“Put your thumb around the top,” said Opa. “Like this.”

After feeding the lamb, Opa took Reese outside.

“Here are some new friends,” said Opa. “This is Ace, the horse, and the cow’s name is Moose.”

After dinner, Reese messaged Dad.

“I miss you,” Reese wrote. “It is nice to spend time with Oma and Opa. And the animals are cute!”

The next morning, Reese helped Oma collect eggs.

"The chickens are called Gnome and Bounce," said Oma. "And this is Bruce the goose."

Reese smiled.

Later, Reese helped Opa make some bread. They used their knuckles to knead the mixture. Opa showed Reese how to put a design on top.

The next day, Reese joined Oma and Bomber on a walk.

Oma was climbing over a gnarled log. Suddenly, she lost her balance.

“My knee!” Oma cried.

Reese helped Oma to sit up carefully.

“Something is wrong,” said Oma. “I hurt my knee and wrist.”

“We need to call Opa,” said Reese.

“I didn’t bring my phone,” sighed Oma.

Reese began to think.

“I know!” Reese said after a moment.

"Bomber!" called Reese. "Run home! Find Opa!"

Bomber barked and ran.

"Find Opa!" Reese called again after him.

A little later, Reese heard the ute. Then they heard Opa's voice.

"Over here!" called Reese.

Opa raced down the track.

Opa made space on the back seat for Oma. Reese wrapped a blanket around her. Opa drove them back to the house.

Later, Reese called Dad.

“Oma has wrenched her knee,” Reese said. “Can I stay longer to help out?”

“Yes, you can,” said Dad.

Dad picked Reese up the next week.

Oma's knee was already feeling much better.

"Reese has been a big help!" said Opa.

"I really love being here," Reese said. "There is so much to do!"

"I knew you would," said Dad.

Bomber barked.

# Look Back

Encourage students to use the pictures to retell the story.